Good Luck Chestnut

And Other Lucky Colors of the World

Look for these other titles by Linda Gruenberg:

The Isa Book 1, Kenda Press 2020

The Isa Book 2, Kenda Press 2020

The Isa Book 3, Kenda Press 2020

The Isa Book 4, Kenda Press 2020

Hummer, Houghton Mifflin Company 1990

ISBN: 978-91-986316-8-5
Imprint: Kenda Press

www.lindagruenberg.com

For my mother, who first sang the lullaby to me with the words, "Dapples and grays, pintos and bays, all those pretty little horses." I have had horse colors in my head ever since—and my mother's loving voice.

Good Luck Chestnut

And other lucky colors of the World

Written and illustrated by Linda Gruenberg

Palomino, jalapeño, maraschino cherry,

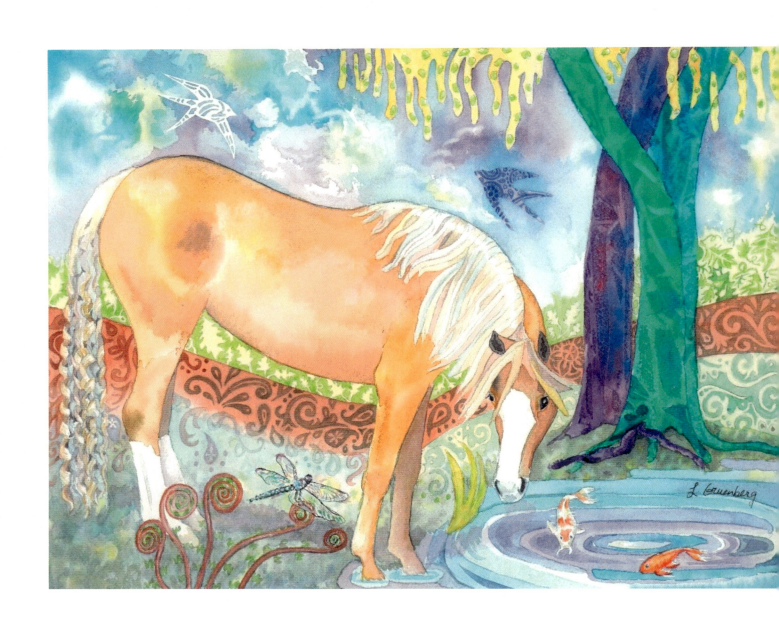

Chestnut, good luck,

goldfish and canaries.

Red roan, blue roan, frosted with crochet,

Chocolate roan, windblown, Hersheys under lace.

Buckskin, mandolin, black-eyed Susan,

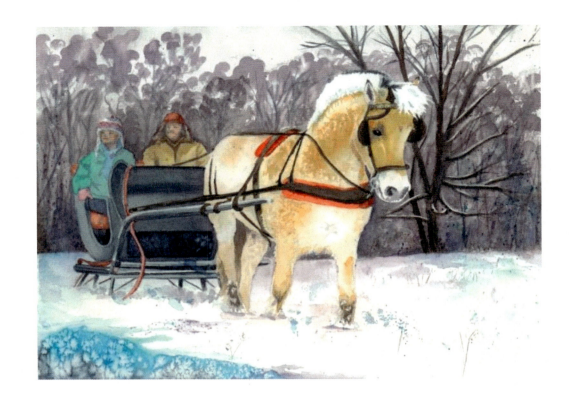

Dun-factor, fun-factor, round mouse snoozin'.

Gray lady, hay baby, dapples in the haze,

Flea-bitten, snowy mittens, freckles in a maze.

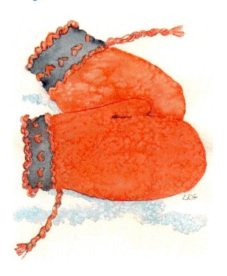

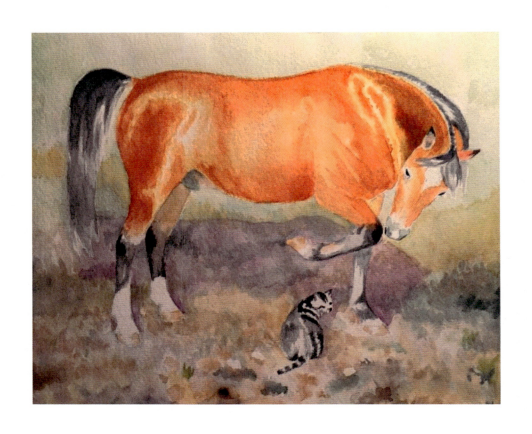

Blood bay, copper bay, shining belly whopper,

Bay baby, hey lady, ruby belly flopper.

Silver dapple, Adam's apple, kick the bucket over,

Cremello, marshmallow, rabbit in the clover.

Linda Gruenberg

Paintbrush, pinto beans, leap-frogging blue jeans,

Paint box, pinto fox, splashed white jelly beans.

Appaloosa, no excuses, blanket on her back,

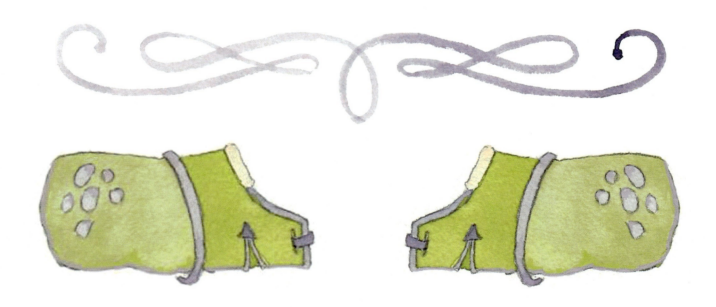

Leopard appy, slap-happy, lacy applejack.

Blazes, swirls, cowlicks lickin',

Stars and stripes and snips for kissin'.

One sock, two socks, triple-sock bedrock,

Flaxen-maned forelock, I rock, you rock.

The End

Can you find examples of the following horse colors and markings?

Appaloosa: Appaloosas have patterns of spots, such as "leopard" where the base color is white with dark spots, and "blanket," where the horse looks like they have a white blanket thrown over their back or rump, with spots on the blanket.

Bay: A bay horse has a coat of red, brown or copper and also has black legs, mane and tail.

Blaze: A blaze is a solid white ribbon down the horse's face.

Buckskin: Buckskins have a gold or tan coat, while their manes, tails, and legs are black.

Chestnut: Chestnuts have a solid red coat which can be anything from a light shade of copper red to a dark shade of liver red. Their manes and tails will either be the same color as the coat or lighter, and even flaxen.

Cremello: Cremellos have creamy coats, white mane and tail, and their skin is pink (especially noticeable around the eyes and muzzle.)

Dapples: Dapples are a faint pattern of lighter-colored spots in a horse's coat.

Dun: The coat can be a variety of shades, but all duns have some of the primitive dun factors such as zebra-like stripes on the legs, cobwebbing on the forehead or throughout the coat, and a dorsal stripe along the spine. Coat colors include bay dun, red dun, yellow dun, and blue dun (also called grulla).

Flaxen: Flaxen is cream-colored, used to describe a horse's mane and tail.

Gray: Horses with a gray gene are born another color and then go gray over time, often in stages. A gray can go through a dapple-gray stage, then gradually become flea-bitten and eventually white. Even white-colored grays are considered gray due to their dark skin.

Paint: Paint is part of the name of a breed registration (American Paint Horse Association, or APHA), a registry for pinto-colored stock-type horses. That means that Paint horses are pintos, but not all pintos are Paints.

Palomino: Palominos have a deep gold or yellow coat with flaxen mane and tail.

Pinto: Pinto is the general term for horses that have large patches of white and any other color.

Roan: Roans have white flecks or ticking in an otherwise solid-colored coat. Roans can come in a variety of base colors, so that "red roan," "strawberry roan," "blue roan," and "chocolate roan" are all possible.

Snip: A snip is a white patch on the horse's muzzle, as small as a spot between the nostrils, or covering the whole nose.

Sock: A sock is what it sounds like: looking as though a horse is wearing a white sock that comes up just past the fetlock.

Splashed white: Splashed white is a type of pinto coloring where the white comes from underneath, as though the horse has splashed through white paint.

Stocking: A stocking is like a sock, but higher, reaching almost to the knee or hock.

Stripe: A stripe is a very narrow blaze down the horse's face.

Acknowledgements

I'M GRATEFUL to Kim Van Der Veer who challenged me to paint the first picture for *Good Luck Chestnut*, and my Craftsy art teacher, Ann Thomas, who literally taught me how to paint children. All the children whose faces are hidden are pre-Ann, and the ones whose faces appear happened during or after Ann's class. Thanks to Carol Holly, my first art teacher, who helped me with depth. She explained how to "push this back, and honey, pull this forward" with my paintbrush. Thanks to my boss, Doug Horning, for giving me my first set of watercolor paints and a hefty supply of paper and encouragement along the way. Thanks to the children who hopped all over their horses' backs, doing tricks and posing for me, like Rose, Deena, Cora, Natalie, Ellie and Nic, and thanks for the children who posed without knowing it, like Vanessa, Annie and Roghayeh, but showed up in my book. Thanks to my friend Sally Ghist who shared information about duns. Thanks to Kenneth for his endless reading and humor. Thanks to the whole Shore to Shore gang of horse-loving, horse-riding friends who egg me on.